Bedtime
Stories

The Lion and The Mouse

A Mouse running over his face awakened a Lion from sleep. Rising up angrily, he caught him and was about to kill him. Then the Mouse piteously entreated, saying: "If you would only spare my life, I would be sure to repay your kindness." The Lion laughed at him but allowed him to go. It happened shortly after this that some hunters, who bound him by strong ropes to the ground, caught the Lion. The Mouse, recognizing his roar, came and gnawed the rope with his teeth, and set him free, exclaiming: "You ridiculed the idea of my ever being able to help you, never expecting to receive from me any repayment of your favor, Now you know that it is possible for even a Mouse to confer benefits on a Lion."

Moral of the story

Never underestimate others

What I learned from the story :

....
....
....
....

A Town Mouse and A Country Mouse

A Town Mouse and a Country Mouse were friends. The Country Mouse one day invited his friend to come and see him at his home in the fields. The Town Mouse came and they sat down to a dinner of barleycorns and roots the latter of which had a distinctly earthy flavour. The flavour was not much to the taste of the guest and presently he broke out with "My poor dear friend, you live here no better than the ants. Now, you should just see how I fare! My larder is a regular horn of plenty. You must come and stay with me and I promise you shall live on the fat of the land." So when he returned to town he took the Country Mouse with him and showed him into a larder containing flour and oatmeal and figs and honey and dates.

The Country Mouse had never seen anything like it and sat down to enjoy the luxuries his friend provided. But before they had well begun, the door of the larder opened and someone came in. The two Mice scampered off and hid themselves in a narrow and exceedingly uncomfortable hole. Presently, when all was quiet, they ventured out again. But someone else came in, and off they scuttled again. This was too much for the visitor. "Good bye," said he, "I'm off. You live in the lap of luxury, I can see, but you are surrounded by dangers whereas at home I can enjoy my simple dinner of roots and corn in peace."

Moral of the story

Safety is the first importance.

What I learned from the story:

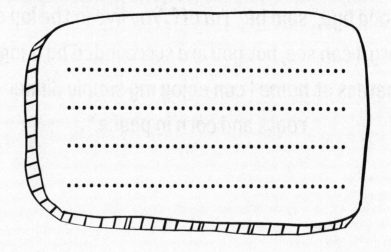

....
....
....
....

Elephant and Friends

One day an elephant wandered into a forest in search of friends. He saw a monkey on a tree. "Will you be my friend?" asked the elephant. Replied the monkey, "You are too big. You can not swing from trees like me." Next, the elephant met a rabbit. He asked him to be his friend. But the rabbit said, "You are too big to play in my burrow!" Then the elephant met a frog. "Will you be my friend? He asked. "How can I?" asked the frog. "You are too big to leap about like me." The elephant was upset. He met a fox next. "Will you be my friend?" he asked the fox. The fox said, "Sorry, sir, you are too big." The next day, the elephant saw all the animals in the forest running for their lives.

The elephant asked them what the matter was. The bear replied, "There is a tier in the forest. He's trying to gobble us all up!" The animals all ran away to hide. The elephant wondered what he could do to solve everyone in the forest. Meanwhile, the tiger kept eating up whoever he could find. The elephant walked up to the tiger and said, "Please, Mr. Tiger, do not eat up these poor animals." "Mind your own business!" growled the tiger. The elephant has a no choice but to give the tiger a hefty kick. The frightened tiger ran for his life. The elephant ambled back into the forest to announce the good news to everyone. All the animals thanked the elephant. They said, "You are just the right size to be our friend."

Moral of the story

Friends come in all shapes and sizes!

What I learned from the story:

....
....
....
....

Four Friends

Once upon a time in a small village lived four Friends named Satyanand, Vidhyanand, Dharmanand and Sivanand. They had grown up together to become good friends. Satyanand, Vidhyanand and Dharmanand were very knowledgeable. But Sivanand spent most of his time eating and sleeping. He was considered foolish by everyone. Once famine struck the village. All the crops failed. Rivers and lakes started to dry up. The people of the villages started moving to other villages to save their lives. "We also need to move to another place soon or else we will also die like many others," said Satyanand. They all agreed with him.

"But what about Sivanand?" Asked Satyanand. "Do we need him with us? He has no skills or knowledge. We cannot take him with us," replied Dharmanand. "He will be a burden on us." "How can we leave him behind? He grew up with us," said Vidhyanand. "We will share what ever we earn equally among the four of us." They all agreed to take Sivanand along with them. They packed all necessary things and set out for a nearby town. On the way, they had to cross a forest. As they were walking through the forest, they came across the bones of an animal. They became curious and stopped to take a closer look at the bones. "Those are the bones of a lion," said Vidhyanand. The others agreed.

"This is a great opportunity to test our knowledge," said Satyanand."I can put the bones together." Saying so, he brought the bones together to form the skeleton of a lion."Dharmanand said, "I can put muscles and tissue on it." Soon a lifeless lion lay before them."I can breathe life into that body." said Vidhyanand.But before he could continue, Sivanand jumped up to stop him. "No. Don't! If you put life into that lion, it will kill us all," he cried. "Oh you coward! You can't stop me from testing my skills and knowledge," shouted an angry Vidhyanand. "You are here with us only because I requested the others to let you come along."

"Then please let me climb that tree first," said a frightened Sivanand running towards the nearest tree. Just as Sivanand pulled himself on to the tallest branch of the tree Vidhyanand brought life into the lion. Getting up with a deafening roar, the lion attacked and killed the three educated friends.

Moral of the story

Sometimes, It is better to be practical than educated.

What I learned from the story:

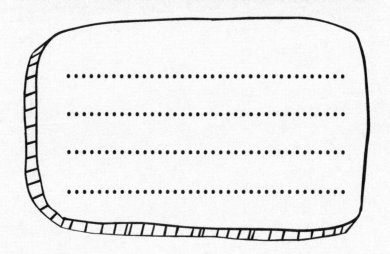

The Ant and The Dove

On a hot day of summer, an ant was searching for some water. After walking around for some time, she came near the river. To drink the water, she climbed up on a small rock. While trying to drink water, she slipped and fell into the river. There was a dove sitting on a branch of a tree who saw the ant falling into the river. The dove quickly plucked a leaf and dropped it into the river near the struggling ant. The ant moved towards the leaf and climbed up onto it. Soon, the leaf drifted to dry ground, and the ant jumped out. She looked up to the tree and thanked the dove.

Later, the same day, a bird catcher nearby was about to throw his net over the dove hoping to trap it. An ant saw him and guessed what he was about to do. The dove was resting and he had no idea about the bird catcher. The ant quickly bit him on the foot. Feeling the pain, the bird catcher dropped his net and let out a light scream. The dove noticed it and quickly flew away.

Moral of the story

You reap what you sow

What I learned from the story :

....
....
....
....

Unity is Strength

Once upon a time, there was a flock of doves that flew in search of food led by their king. One day, they had flown a long distance and were very tired. The dove king encouraged them to fly a little further. The smallest dove picked up speed and found some rice scattered beneath a banyan tree. So all the doves landed and began to eat. Suddenly a net fell over them and they were all trapped. They saw a hunter approaching carrying a huge club. The doves desperately fluttered their wings trying to get out, but to no avail. The king had an idea. He advised all the doves to fly up together carrying the net with them. He said that there was strength in unity.

Each dove picked up a portion of the net and together they flew off carrying the net with them. The hunter looked up in astonishment. He tried to follow them, but they were flying high over hills and valleys. They flew to a hill near a city of temples where there lived a mouse who could help them. He was a faithful friend of the dove king. When the mouse heard the loud noise of their approach, he went into hiding. The dove king gently called out to him and then the mouse was happy to see him. The dove king explained that they had been caught in a trap and needed the mouse's help to gnaw at the net with his teeth and set them free.

The mouse agreed saying that he would set the king free first. The king insisted that he first free his subjects and the king last. The mouse understood the king's feelings and complied with his wishes. He began to cut the net and one by one all the doves were freed including the dove king. They all thanked the mouse and flew away together, united in their strength.

Moral of the story

When you work together, you are stronger.

What I learned from the story:

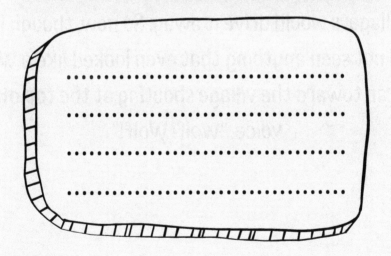

The Shepherd Boy and the Wolf

A Shepherd Boy tended his master's Sheep near a dark forest not far from the village. Soon he found life in the pasture very dull. All he could do to amuse himself was to talk to his dog or play on his shepherd's pipe. One day as he sat watching the Sheep and the quiet forest, and thinking what he would do should he see a Wolf, he thought of a plan to amuse himself. His Master had told him to call for help should a Wolf attack the flock, and the Villagers would drive it away. So now, though he had not seen anything that even looked like a Wolf, he ran toward the village shouting at the top of his voice, "Wolf! Wolf!"

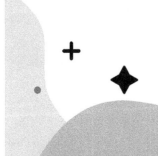

As he expected, the Villagers who heard the cry dropped their work and ran in great excitement to the pasture. But when they got there they found the Boy doubled up with laughter at the trick he had played on them. A few days later the Shepherd Boy again shouted, "Wolf! Wolf!" Again the Villagers ran to help him, only to be laughed at again. Then one evening as the sun was setting behind the forest and the shadows were creeping out over the pasture, a Wolf really did spring from the underbrush and fall upon the Sheep. In terror the Boy ran toward the village shouting "Wolf! Wolf!" But though the Villagers heard the cry, they did not run to help him as they had before. "He cannot fool us again," they said. The Wolf killed a great many of the Boy's sheep and then slipped away into the forest.

Moral of the story

If you keep lying, no one will believe you even if you are speaking the truth. Always speak the truth.

What I learned from the story :

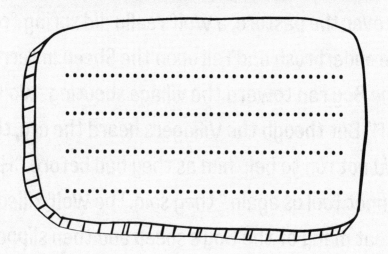

The Lion and the Clever Fox

Long ago, there lived a lion in a dense forest. One morning his wife told him that his breath was bad and unpleasant. The lion became embarrassed and angry upon hearing it. He wanted to check this fact with others. So he called three others outside his cave. First came the sheep. The Lion opening his mouth wide said, "Sheep, tell me if my mouth smells bad?" The sheep thought that the lion wanted an honest answer, so the sheep said, "Yes, Friend. There seems to be something wrong with your breath". This plain speak did not go well with the lion. He pounced on the sheep, killing it.

Then the lion called the wolf and said, "What do you think? Do I have a bad breath?" The wolf saw what happened to the sheep. He wanted to be very cautious in answering a question. So, the wolf said, "Who says that Your breath is unpleasant. It's as sweet as the smell of roses". When the lion heard the reply, he roared in an anger and immediately attacked the wolf and killed it. "The flatterer!" growled the lion. Finally, came the turn of the fox. The lion asked him the same question. The fox was well aware of the fate of the sheep and the wolf. So he coughed and cleared his throat again and again and then said, "Oh Dear Friend, for the last few days, I have been having a very bad cold. Due to this, I can't smell anything, pleasant or unpleasant". The lion spared the fox's life.

Moral of the story

Sometimes, It's wise to stay away from certain situations.

What I learned from the story :

....
....
....
....

The Wolf and the Crane

A Wolf had been feasting too greedily, and a bone had stuck crosswise in his throat. He could get it neither up nor down, and of course, he could not eat a thing. Naturally, that was an awful state of affairs for a greedy Wolf. So away he hurried to the Crane. He was sure that she, with her long neck and bill, would easily be able to reach the bone and pull it out. "I will reward you very handsomely", said the Wolf, "if you pull that bone out for me". The Crane, as you can imagine, was very uneasy about putting her head in Wolf's throat. But she was grasping in nature, so she did what the Wolf asked her to do. When the Wolf felt that the bone was gone, he started to walk away.

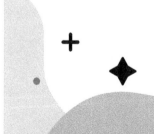

"But what about my reward!" called the Crane anxiously. "What!" snarled the Wolf, whirling around. "Haven't you got it? Isn't it enough that I let you take your head out of my mouth without snapping it off?"

Moral of the story

Staying in a company of selfish people will not do anyone any favor.

What I learned from the story :

....
....
....
....

The Pig and The Sheep

One day a shepherd discovered a fat Pig in the meadow where his Sheep were pastured. He very quickly captured the porker, which squealed at the top of its voice the moment the Shepherd laid his hands on it. You would have thought, to hear the loud squealing, that the Pig was being cruelly hurt. But in spite of its squeals and struggles to escape, the Shepherd tucked his prize under his arm and started off to the butcher's in the marketplace. The Sheep in the pasture were much astonished and amused at the Pig's behavior and followed the Shepherd and his charge to the pasture gate.

"What makes you squeal like that?" asked one of the Sheep. "The Shepherd often catches and carries off one of us. But we should feel very much ashamed to make such a terrible fuss about it like you do." "That is all very well," replied the Pig, with a squeal and a frantic kick. "When he catches you he is only after your wool. But he wants my bacon! gree-ee-ee!"

Moral of the story

It is easy to be brave when there is no danger

What I learned from the story :

....
....
....
....

The Man and the Lion

A Lion and a Man chanced to travel in a company through the forest. They soon began to quarrel, for each of them boasted that he and his kind were far superior to the other both in strength and mind. Now they reached a clearing in the forest and there stood a statue. It was a representation of Heracles in the act of tearing the jaws of the Nemean Lion. "See," said the man, "that's how strong we are! The King of Beasts is like wax in our hands!" "Ho!" laughed the Lion, "a Man made that statue. It would have been quite a different scene had a Lion made it!"

Moral of the story

Always trust your own wit

What I learned from the story :

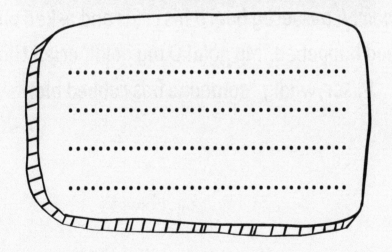

Wealth without a Value

A Miser had buried his gold in a secret place in his garden. Every day he went to the spot, dug up the treasure and counted it piece by piece to make sure it was all there. He made so many trips that a Thief, who had been observing him, guessed what it was the Miser had hidden, and one night quietly dug up the treasure and made off with it. When the Miser discovered his loss, he was overcome with grief and despair. He groaned and cried and tore his hair. A passerby heard his cries and asked what had happened. "My gold! O my gold!" cried the Miser, wildly, "someone has robbed me!"

"Your gold! There in that hole? Why did you put it there? Why did you not keep it in the house where you could easily get it when you had to buy things?" "Buy!" screamed the Miser angrily. "Why, I never touched the gold. I couldn't think of spending any of it." The stranger picked up a large stone and threw it into the hole. "If that is the case," he said, "cover up that stone. It is worth just as much to you as the treasure you lost!"

Moral of the story

> A possession is worth no more than the use we make of it.

What I learned from the story :

....
....
....
....

The Woodcutter and the Axe

Long ago, there lived a woodcutter in a small village. He was sincere in his work and very honest. Every day, he set out into the nearby forest to cut trees. He brought the woods back into the village and sold them out to a merchant and earn his money. He earned just about enough to make a living, but he was satisfied with his simple living.One day, while cutting a tree near a river, his axe slipped out of his hand and fell into the river. The river was so deep, he could not even think to retrieve it on his own. He only had one axe which was gone into the river. He became very worried thinking how he will be able to earn his living now! He was very sad and prayed to the Goddess.

He prayed sincerely so the Goddess appeared in front of him and asked, "What is the problem, my son?" The woodcutter explained the problem and requested the Goddess to get his axe back. The Goddess put her hand deep into the river and took out a silver axe and asked, "Is this your axe?" The Woodcutter looked at the axe and said "No". So the Goddess put her hand back deep into the water again and showed a golden axe and asked, "Is this your axe?" The woodcutter looked at the axe and said "No". The Goddess said, "Take a look again Son, this is a very valuable golden axe, are you sure this is not yours?" The woodcutter said, "No, It's not mine. I can't cut the trees with a golden axe. It's not useful for me".

The Goddess smiled and finally put her hand into the water again and took out his iron axe and asked, "Is this your axe?" To this, the woodcutter said, "Yes! This is mine! Thank you!" The Goddess was very impressed with his honesty so she gave him his iron axe and also other two axes as a reward for his honesty.

Moral of the story

Always be honest. Honesty is always rewarded.

What I learned from the story :

....
....
....
....

The Priest and The Goat

Once, there lived a pious Priest in a small village. He was very innocent and simple minded person, used to perform religious rituals. On one occasion, he was rewarded with the goat for his services by a wealthy man. The Priest was happy to get a goat as the reward. He happily slung the goat over his shoulder and began the journey towards his home. On the way, three cheats (Thugs) saw the Priest taking the goat. All of them were lazy and wanted to cheat the Priest so that they could take away the goat. They said, "This goat will make a delicious meal for all of us. Let's somehow get it".

They discussed the matter amongst themselves and devised a plan to get the goat by fooling the Priest. After deciding the plan, they got separated from one another and took different hiding positions at three different places on the way of the Priest. As soon as, the Priest arrived at a lonely place, one of the cheats came out of his hiding place and asked Priest in a shocking manner, "Sir, what are you doing? I don't understand why a pious man like you needs to carry a dog on his shoulders?" The Priest was surprised to hear such words. He screamed, "Can't you see? It's not a dog but a goat, you stupid fool". The cheat replied, "Sir, I beg your pardon. I told you what I saw. I am sorry if you don't believe it". The Priest was annoyed at the discrepancy but started his journey once again.

The Priest had barely walked a distance, when another cheat came out of his hiding place and asked the Priest, "Sir, why do you carry a dead calf on your shoulders? You seem to be a wise person. Such an act is pure stupidity on your part". The Priest yelled, "What? How can you mistake a living goat for a dead calf?" The second cheat replied, "Sir, you seem to be highly mistaken in this regard. Either you don't know how does goat look like or you are doing it knowingly. I just told you what I saw. Thank you". The second cheat went away smiling. The Priest got confused but continued to walk further.

Again the Priest had covered a little distance when the third cheat met him. The third cheat asked laughingly, "Sir, why do you carry a donkey on your shoulders? It makes you a laughing stock". Hearing the words of the third thug, the Priest became really worried. He started thinking, "Is it really not a goat? Is it some kind of a ghost?" He thought that the animal he was carrying on his shoulders might really be some sort of ghost, because it transformed itself from the goat into a dog, from a dog into a dead calf and from dead calf into a donkey. The Priest got frightened to such an extent that he hurled the goat on the roadside and ran away. The three tricksters laughed at the gullible Priest. They caught the goat and were happy to feast on it.

Moral of the story

One should not be carried away by what others say.

What I learned from the story :

....
....
....
....

Farmer's Well & Witty Birbal

Once a man sold his well to a farmer. Next day when the farmer went to draw the water from that well, the man did not allow him to draw the water from it. He said, "I have sold you the well, not the water, so you cannot draw the water from the well." The farmer became very sad and came to the Emperor's court. He described everything to the Emperor and asked for justice. The Emperor called Birbal and handed over this case to him. Birbal called the man who sold the well to the farmer. Birbal asked, "Why don't you let him use the water of the well. You have sold the well to the farmer." The man replied, "Birbal, I have sold the well to the farmer, not the water. He has no right to draw the water from the well."

Then Birbal smiled and said to him, "Good, but look, since you have sold the well to this farmer, and you claim that water is yours, then you have no right to keep your water in the farmer's well. Either you pay rent to the farmer to keep your water in his well, or you take that out of his well immediately." The man understood, that his trick has failed. Birbal has outwitted him.

Moral of the story

> Don't Try to Cheat. You will end up paying for it regardless of how smart you think you are.

What I learned from the story:

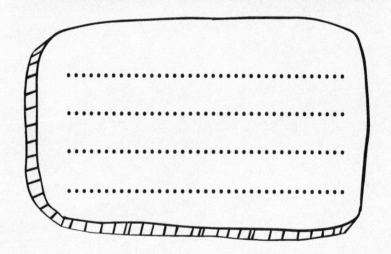

The Fox and The Goat

Once a fox was roaming around in the dark. Unfortunately, he fell into a well. He tried his best to come out but all in vain. So, he had no other alternative but to remain there until the next morning. The next day, a goat came that way. She peeped into the well and saw the fox there. The goat asked, "what are you doing there, Mr. Fox?" The sly fox replied, "I came here to drink water. It is the best I have ever tasted. Come and see for yourself." Without thinking even for a while, the goat jumped into the well, quenched her thirst and looked for a way to get out. But just like the fox, she also found herself helpless to come out.

Then the fox said, "I have an idea. You stand on your hind legs. I'll climb on your head and get out. Then I shall help you come out too." The goat was innocent enough to understand the shrewdness of the fox and did as the fox said and helped him get out of the well. While walking away, the fox said, "Had you been intelligent enough, you would never have got in without seeing how to get out."

Moral of the story

Look before you leap. Do not just blindly walk in to anything without thinking.

What I learned from the story :

....
....
....
....

The Golden Egg

Once upon a time, there lived a cloth merchant in a village with his wife and two children. They were indeed quite well-off. They had a beautiful hen which laid an egg every day. It was not an ordinary egg, rather, a golden egg. But the man was not satisfied with what he used to get daily. He was a get rich-trice kind of a person. The man wanted to get all the golden eggs from his hen at one single go. So, one day he thought hard and at last clicked upon a plan. He decided to kill the hen and get all the eggs together.

So, the next day when the hen laid a golden egg, the man caught hold of it, took a sharp knife, chopped off its neck and cut its body open. There was nothing but blood all around & no trace of any egg at all. He was highly grieved because now he would not get even one single egg. His life was going on smoothly with one egg a day but now, he himself made his life miserable. The outcome of his greed was that he started becoming poorer & poorer day by day and ultimately became a pauper. How jinxed and how much foolish he was.

Moral of the story

One who desires more, loses all.

What I learned from the story :

....
....
....
....

The Bear and The Two Friends

Once two friends were walking through the forest. They knew that anything dangerous can happen to them at any time in the forest. So they promised each other that they would remain united in any case of danger. Suddenly, they saw a large bear approaching them. One of the friends at once climbed a nearby tree. But the other one did not know how to climb. So being led by his common sense, he lay down on the ground breathless, pretending to be a dead man.

The bear came near the man lying on the ground. It smelt in his ears, and slowly left the place. Because the bears do not touch the dead creatures. Now the friend on the tree came down and asked his friend on the ground, "Friend, what did the bear tell you into your ears?" The other friend replied, "The bear advised me not to believe a false friend."

Moral of the story

> **True Friend is the one who always supports and stands by you in any situation.**

What I learned from the story :

....
....
....
....

The Three Questions

King Akbar was very fond of Birbal. This made a certain courtier very jealous. Now this courtier always wanted to be chief minister, but this was not possible as Birbal filled that position. One day Akbar praised Birbal in front of the courtier. This made the courtier very angry and he said that the king praised Birbal unjustly and if Birbal could answer three of his questions, he would accept the fact that Birbal was intelligent. Akbar always wanting to test Birbals wit readily agreed.

The three questions were
1. How many stars are there in the sky
2. Where is the centre of the Earth
3. How many men and how many women are there in the world.

Immediately Akbar asked Birbal the three questions and informed him that if he could not answer them, he would have to resign as chief minister. To answer the first question, Birbal brought a hairy sheep and said, "There are as many stars in the sky as there is hair on the sheep's body. My friend the courtier is welcome to count them if he likes." To answer the second question, Birbal drew a couple of lines on the floor and bore an iron rod in it and said, "this is the center of the Earth, the courtier may measure it himself if he has any doubts."

In answer to the third question, Birbal said, "Counting the exact number of men and women in the world would be a problem as there are some specimens like our courtier friend here who cannot easily be classified as either. Therefore if all people like him are killed, then and only then can one count the exact number."

Moral of the story

There is Always a Way.

What I learned from the story :

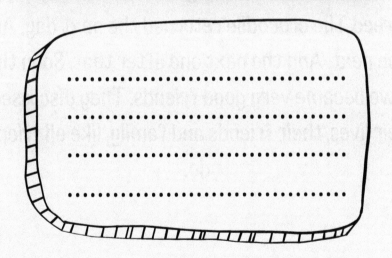

The Monkey and The Crocodile

Once upon a time, a clever monkey lived in a tree that bore juicy, red rose apples. He was very happy. One fine day, a crocodile swam up to that tree and told the monkey that he had traveled a long distance and was in search of food as he was very hungry. The kind monkey offered him a few rose apples. The crocodile enjoyed them very much and asked the monkey whether he could come again for some more fruit. The generous monkey happily agreed. The crocodile returned the next day. And the next. And the next one after that. Soon the two became very good friends. They discussed their lives, their friends and family, like all friends do.

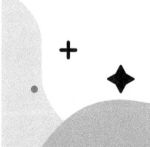

The crocodile told the monkey that he had a wife and that they lived on the other side of the river. So the kind monkey offered him some extra rose apples to take home to his wife. The crocodile's wife loved the rose apples and made her husband promise to get her some every day. Meanwhile, the friendship between the monkey and the crocodile deepened as they spent more and more time together. The crocodile's wife started getting jealous. She wanted to put an end to this friendship.

So she pretended that she could not believe that her husband could be friends with a monkey. Her husband tried to convince her that he and the monkey shared a true friendship. The crocodile's wife thought to herself that if the monkey lived on a diet of rose monkeys, his flesh would be very sweet. So she asked the crocodile to invite the monkey to their house. The crocodile was not happy about this. He tried to make the excuse that it would be difficult to get the monkey across the river. But his wife was determined to eat the monkey's flesh. So she thought of a plan.

One day, she pretended to be very ill and told the crocodile that the doctor said that she would only recover if she ate a monkey's heart. If her husband wanted to save her life, he must bring her his friend's heart. The crocodile was aghast. He was in a dilemma. On the one hand, he loved his friend. On the other, he could not possibly let his wife die. The crocodile's wife threatened him saying that if he did not get her the monkey's heart, she would surely die. So the crocodile went to the rose apple tree and invited the monkey to come home to meet his wife. He told the monkey that he could ride across the river on the crocodile's back. The monkey happily agreed.

As they reached the middle of the river, the crocodile began to sink. The frightened monkey asked him why he was doing that. The crocodile explained that he would have to kill the monkey to save his wife's life. The clever monkey told him that he would gladly give up his heart to save the life of the crocodile's wife, but he had left his heart behind in the rose apple tree. He asked the crocodile to make haste and turn back so that the monkey could go get his heart from the apple tree. The silly crocodile quickly swam back to the rose apple tree. The monkey scampered up the tree to safety. He told the crocodile to tell his wicked wife that she had married the biggest fool in the world.

Moral of the story

Don't underestimate yourself. There are bigger fools in this world.

What I learned from the story:

....
....
....
....

The Little Mouse

Once upon a time, there was a Baby Mouse and Mother Mouse. They lived in a hole in the skirting board in a big, warm house with lots of cheese to eat, where they wanted for nothing. Then, one day, Mother Mouse decided to take Baby Mouse outside of their home. Waiting outside for them was a huge ginger tomcat, licking its lips and waiting to eat them both up. "Mother, Mother! What should we do?" Cried Baby Mouse, clinging to his mother's tail. Mother Mouse paused, staring up into the beady eyes of the hungry cat. But she wasn't scared because she knew exactly how to deal with big, scary cats. She opened her mouth and took in a deep breath.

"Woof! Woof! Bark bark bark!" She shouted, and the cat ran away as fast as he could. "Wow, Mother! That was amazing!" Baby Mouse said to his mother, smiling happily. "And that, my child, is why it is always best to have a second language."

Moral of the story

It's always good to have a second language.

What I learned from the story :

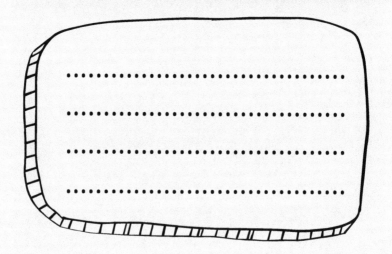

The Fox and the Grapes

One afternoon a fox was walking through the forest and spotted a bunch of grapes hanging from over a lofty branch. "Just the thing to quench my thirst," he thought. Taking a few steps back, the fox jumped and just missed the hanging grapes. Again the fox took a few paces back and tried to reach them but still failed. Finally, giving up, the fox turned up his nose and said, "They're probably sour anyway," and proceeded to walk away.

Moral of the story

It's easy to despise what you cannot have. Nothing comes easy without hard work. So, Work Hard and reach your goals.

What I learned from the story :

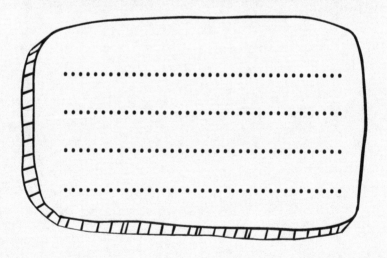

The Rabbit and the Turtle

One day a rabbit was boasting about how fast he could run. He was laughing at the turtle for being so slow. Much to the rabbit's surprise, the turtle challenged him to a race. The rabbit thought this was a good joke and accepted the challenge. The fox was to be the umpire of the race. As the race began, the rabbit raced way ahead of the turtle, just like everyone thought. The rabbit got to the halfway point and could not see the turtle anywhere.

He was hot and tired and decided to stop and take a short nap. Even if the turtle passed him, he would be able to race to the finish line ahead of him. All this time the turtle kept walking step by step by step. He never quit no matter how hot or tired he got. He just kept going.However, the rabbit slept longer than he had thought and woke up. He could not see the turtle anywhere! He went at full speed to the finish line but found the turtle there waiting for him.

Moral of the story

Never underestimate the weakest opponent.

What I learned from the story :

....
....
....
....

Lion and His Fear

There was a lion who feared nothing except the crowing of cocks. A chill would go down his spine whenever he heard a cock crowing. One day he confessed his fear to the elephant, who was greatly amused. "How can the crowing of a cock hurt you?" he asked the lion. "Think about it!" Just then a mosquito began circling the elephant's head, frightening him out of his wits. "If it gets into my ear I'm doomed!" he shrieked, flailing at the insect with his trunk. Now it was the lion's turn to feel amused.

Moral of the story

If we could see our fears as others see them we would realize that most of our fears make no sense!

What I learned from the story :

....
....
....
....

The Farmer and the Snake

A Farmer walked through his field one cold winter morning. On the ground lay a Snake, stiff and frozen with the cold. The Farmer knew how deadly the Snake could be, and yet he picked it up and put it in his bosom to warm it back to life. The Snake soon revived, and when it had enough strength, bit the man who had been so kind to it. The bite was deadly and the Farmer felt that he must die. As he drew his last breath, he said to those standing around, "Learn from my fate not to take pity on a scoundrel".

Moral of the story

There are some who never change their nature, regardless of how good we behave with them.

What I learned from the story:

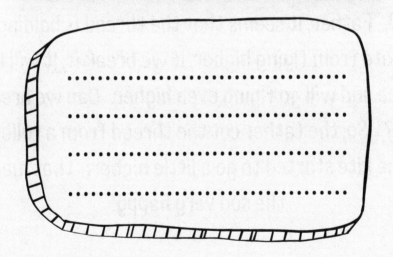

The Kite without a thread

Once a father and son went to the kite flying festival. The young son became very happy seeing the sky filled with colorful kites. He too asked his father to get him a kite and a thread with a roller so he can fly a kite too. So, the father went to the shop at the park where the festival was being held. He purchased kites and a roll of thread for his son. His son started to fly a kite. Soon, his kite reached high up in the sky. After a while, the son said, "Father, It seems that the thread is holding up a kite from flying higher, If we break it, It will be free and will go flying even higher. Can we break it?" So, the father cut the thread from a roller. The kite started to go a little higher. That made the son very happy.

But then, slowly, the kite started to come down. And, soon it fell down on the terrace of an unknown building. The young son was surprised to see this. He had cut the kite loose of its thread so it can fly higher, but instead, it fell down. He asked his father, "Father, I thought that after cutting off the thread, the kite can freely fly higher. But why did it fall down?" The Father explained, "Son, At the height of life that we live in, we often think that some things we are tied with and they are preventing us from going further higher.

The thread was not holding the kite from going higher, but it was helping it stay higher when the wind slowed down and when the wind picked up, you helped the kite go up higher in a proper direction through the thread. And when we cut the thread, it fell down without the support you were providing to the kite through the thread". The son realized his mistake.

Moral of the story

Never let go of your family, They are the ones supporting you, not the ones holding you back.

What I learned from the story:

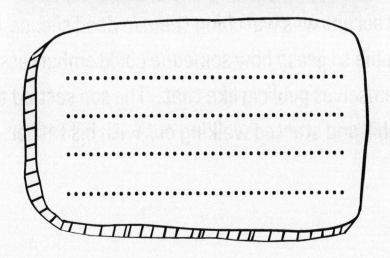

Evening Dinner with a Father

A son took his old father to a restaurant for an evening dinner. Father being very old and weak, while eating, dropped food on his shirt and trousers. Other diners watched him in disgust while his son was calm. After he finished eating, his son who was not at all embarrassed, quietly took him to the washroom, wiped the food particles, removed the stains, combed his hair and fitted his spectacles firmly. When they came out, the entire restaurant was watching them in dead silence, not able to grasp how someone could embarrass themselves publicly like that. The son settled the bill and started walking out with his father.

At that time, an old man amongst the diners called out to the son and asked him, "Don't you think you have left something behind?". The son replied, "No sir, I haven't". The old man retorted, "Yes, you have! You left a lesson for every son and hope for every father". The restaurant went silent.

Moral of the story

To care for those who once cared for us is one of the highest honors.

What I learned from the story:

....
....
....
....

Making Relations Special

When I was a kid, my Mom liked to make breakfast food for dinner every now and then. And I remember one night in particular when she had made dinner after a long, hard day at work. On that evening so long ago, my Mom placed a plate of eggs, sausage and extremely burned biscuits in front of my dad. I remember waiting to see if anyone noticed! Yet all dad did was reached for his biscuit, smile at my Mom and ask me how my day was at school. I don't remember what I told him that night, but I do remember watching him smear butter and jelly on that biscuit and eat every bite!

When I got up from the table that evening, I remember hearing my Mom apologize to my dad for burning the biscuits. And I'll never forget what he said: "Honey, I love burned biscuits." Later that night, I went to kiss Daddy good night and I asked him if he really liked his biscuits burned. He wrapped me in his arms and said, "Your Momma put in a hard day at work today and she's real tired. And besides – a little burned biscuit never hurt anyone!"

Moral of the story

learning to accept each others faults is one of the most important keys to creating a healthy relationship.

What I learned from the story :

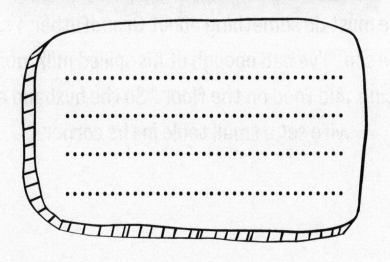

Grandpa's Table

A frail old man went to live with his son, daughter-in-law, and four-year-old grandson. The old man's hands trembled, his eyesight was blurred, and his step faltered. The family ate together at the table. But the elderly grandfather's shaky hands and failing sight made eating difficult. Peas rolled off his spoon onto the floor. When he grasped, the glass, milk spilled on the tablecloth. The son and daughter-in-law became irritated with the mess. "We must do something about Grandfather," said the son. "I've had enough of his spilled milk, noisy eating, and food on the floor." So the husband and wife set a small table in the corner.

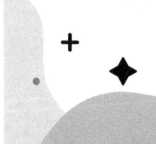

There, Grandfather ate alone while the rest of the family enjoyed dinner. Since Grandfather had broken a dish or two, his food was served in a wooden bowl. When the family glanced in Grandfather's direction, sometimes he had a tear in his eye as he sat alone. Still, the only words the couple had for him were sharp admonitions when he dropped a fork or spilled food. The four-year-old watched it all in silence. One evening before supper, the father noticed his son playing with wood scraps on the floor. He asked the child sweetly, "What are you making?" Just as sweetly, the boy responded, "Oh, I am making a little bowl for you and Mama to eat your food in when I grow up."

The four-year-old smiled and went back to work. The words so struck the parents that they were speechless. Then tears started to stream down their cheeks. Though no word was spoken, both knew what must be done. That evening the husband took Grandfather's hand and gently led him back to the family table. For the remainder of his days, he ate every meal with the family. And for some reason, neither husband nor wife seemed to care any longer when a fork was dropped, milk spilled, or the tablecloth soiled.

Moral of the story

Life is about people connecting with people, and making a positive difference.

What I learned from the story :

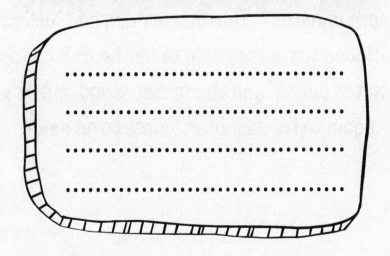

Five More Minutes

While at the park one day, a woman sat down next to a man on a bench near a playground. "That's my son over there," she said, pointing to a little boy in a red sweater who was gliding down the slide. "He's a fine looking boy", the man said. "That's my daughter on the bike in the white dress." Then, looking at his watch, he called to his daughter. "What do you say we go, Melissa?" Melissa pleaded, "Just five more minutes, Dad. Please? Just five more minutes." The man nodded and Melissa continued to ride her bike to her heart's content. Minutes passed and the father stood and called again to his daughter. "Time to go now?"

Again Melissa pleaded, "Five more minutes, Dad. Just five more minutes." The man smiled and said, "OK." "My, you certainly are a patient father," the woman responded. The man smiled and then said, "Her older brother Tommy was killed by a drunk driver last year while he was riding his bike near here. I never spent much time with Tommy and now I'd give anything for just five more minutes with him. I've vowed not to make the same mistake with Melissa. She thinks she has five more minutes to ride her bike. The truth is, I get Five more minutes to watch her play."

Moral of the story

Life is all about making priorities, and family is one and only priority on top of all other, so spend all time you can with loved ones.

What I learned from the story :

SHORT STORIES

CONTENTS

2 THE LION AND THE MOUSE

4 A TOWN MOUSE AND A COUNTRY MOUSE

7 ELEPHANT AND FRIENDS

10 FOUR FRIENDS

15 THE ANT AND THE DOVE

18 UNITY IS STRENGTH

22 THE SHEPHERD BOY AND THE WOLF

25 THE LION AND A CLEVER FOX

28 THE WOLF AND THE CRANE

31 THE PIG AND THE SHEEP

34 THE MAN AND THE LION

36 WEALTH WITHOUT A VALUE

39 THE WOODCUTTER AND THE AXE

43 THE PRIEST AND THE GOAT

48 FARMER'S WELL & WITTY BIRBAL

51 THE FOX AND THE GOAT

54 THE GOLDEN EGG

57 THE BEAR AND THE TWO FRIENDS

60 THE THREE QUESTIONS

64 THE MONKEY AND THE CROCODILE

70 THE LITTLE MOUSE

73 THE FOX AND THE GRAPES

75 THE RABBIT AND THE TURTLE

78 LION AND HIS FEAR

80 THE FARMER AND THE SNAKE

82 THE KITE WITHOUT A THREAD

86 EVENING DINNER WITH A FATHER

89 MAKING RELATIONS SPECIAL

92 GRANDPA'S TABLE

96 FIVE MORE MINUTES

The end

Printed in the USA
CPSIA information can be obtained
at www.ICGtesting.com
LVHW022304031224
798267LV00042B/1577